Learning About the Settlement of the Americas with Graphic Organizers

Linda Wirkner

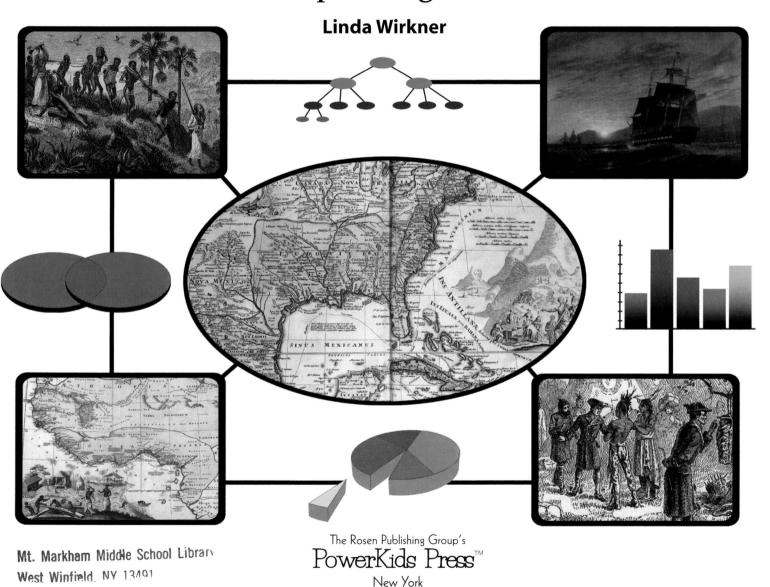

The Rosen Publishing Group's
PowerKids Press™
New York

For Jim whose support never wavers

Published in 2005 by The Rosen Publishing Group, Inc.
29 East 21st Street, New York, NY 10010

First Edition

Editor: Orli Zuravicky
Book Design: Michael Caroleo

Photo Credits: Cover and title page (center), © CORBIS; cover and title page (top left), p. 15 (bottom) Picture Collection, The Branch Libraries, New York Public Library Astor Lenox and Tilden Foundations; cover and title page (top right), p. 8 (bottom left) © Christie's Images/CORBIS; cover and title page (bottom left), p. 15 (top) Library of Congress Geography and Map Division; cover and title page (bottom right), p.19 © Bettmann/CORBIS; pp. 7, 8 (top left) © North Wind Picture Archive; p. 8 (top right) © David Ball/CORBIS; p. 8 (bottom middle right) © Archive Iconografico, S.A./CORBIS; p. 8 (bottom right) © Lindsay Hebberd/CORBIS; p16 bottom) © Joseph Sohm; ChromoSohm Inc./CORBIS.

Library of Congress Cataloging-in-Publication Data

Wirkner, Linda.
Learning about the settlement of the Americas with graphic organizers / Linda Wirkner.
    v. cm. — (Graphic organizers in social studies)
Includes bibliographical references and index.
Contents: Three worlds meet — The first Americans — Columbus's voyage and Spanish exploration — Early English, French, and Dutch exploration — The early English colonies — The trans-atlantic slave trade — Three worlds meet in New York — Life in the new world — Slavery in the colonies — The new Americas.
ISBN 1-4042-2814-4 (lib. bdg.)
ISBN 1-4042-5057-3 (paperback)
1. America—History—To 1810—Juvenile literature. 2. America—Discovery and exploration—Juvenile literature. 3. Indians—History—Juvenile literature. 4. African Americans—History—To 1863—Juvenile literature. 5. Graphic methods—Juvenile literature. [1. America—History—To 1810. 2. America—Discovery and exploration. 3. Indians of North America—History. 4. African Americans—History—To 1863.] I. Title.
E18.82.W57 2005
970.01—dc22

                                    2003022462

Manufactured in the United States of America

Contents

Three Worlds Meet   5

The First Americans   6

Columbus's Voyage and Spanish Exploration   9

Early English, French, and Dutch Exploration   10

The Early English Colonies   13

The Slave Trade   14

Three Worlds Meet in New York   17

Europeans and Native Americans   18

Slavery in the Colonies   21

The New Americas   22

Glossary   23

Index   24

Web Sites   24

Venn Diagram: Three Worlds Meet

Europeans

Native Americans

Africans

- Were interested in wealth and power
- Were interested in colonization and believed that land could be owned
- Practiced Christian religions, including Catholicism and Protestantism
- Wanted to spread Christianity to other peoples and believed that it was the best religion

- Believed that education was important
- Came to North America willingly, and remained there

- Practiced religions based on forces of nature and myths
- Believed that land could not be owned
- Did not have much use for money, and traded goods instead
- Lived off of the land
- Traveled a lot and did not always stay in the same place for long periods of time

- Felt religion was important
- Practiced religions that were based on there being one major god or higher power
- Had forms of upper, middle and lower classes for people in the community
- Were interested in art and created different forms, including painting and pottery

- Used forms of slavery
- Majority of countries were ruled by kings
- Had similar urban communities that traded gold, ivory, and furs, and that were interested in money and wealth

- Shared similar types of ceremonies, which included singing and dancing,
- Passed folk tales and myths down by mouth
- Felt the family unit was very important

- Had 6 types of people in the community: hunter-gatherers, cattle herders, forest dwellers, fishermen, grain raisers, and city/urban
- Practiced traditional African religions and Islam

4

Three Worlds Meet

The first people to live in the Americas crossed over the Bering Land Bridge from Asia thousands of years ago. They settled on land that would later become South America, the Caribbean, Canada, and the United States. They lived there without **contact** from the European world until the 1400s. Then, European **explorers** reached America while looking for a sea route to Asia. This opened the Americas, or the **New World**, to European **colonization**. The first Americans had a lifestyle that was different from that of the Europeans. The two **cultures** often **clashed**. In 1619, another culture was added when African slaves were brought to the Americas. The history of the United States begins with these three worlds meeting. **Graphic organizers** are tools that help you to group ideas. In this book, graphic organizers will help you understand the settlement of the Americas.

A Venn diagram shows how things are alike and how they are different. Each circle tells facts about a different subject. The parts of the circles that overlap show what the subjects have in common. This Venn diagram compares the three different cultures that met in the Americas.

The First Americans

Scientists believe the first Americans arrived on the **continent** of North America between 10,000 and 50,000 years ago. By the 1400s, there were about 650 different groups of people living in the Americas, each with its own language and culture. The Incas, the Maya, and the Aztecs, as they are called today, settled in Central America and South America. Other people settled mostly in what today is the United States. These Native Americans lived off the land. Aside from hunting animals for food, they fished in the rivers, gathered berries and nuts, and farmed the land. When Europeans came to the Americas, they claimed the land for their countries. Unlike the Europeans, Native Americans did not believe that the land could be owned. In the end, all of the native peoples living in the Americas were forced to give up the land that they had called home for thousands of years.

A line graph is a graphic organizer that is used to show a change in something over a period of time. This line graph shows the number of Native Americans living in the Americas both before and after the Europeans arrived. It shows that millions of Native Americans had died by the year 1900.

Line Graph: Native American Populations in the New World

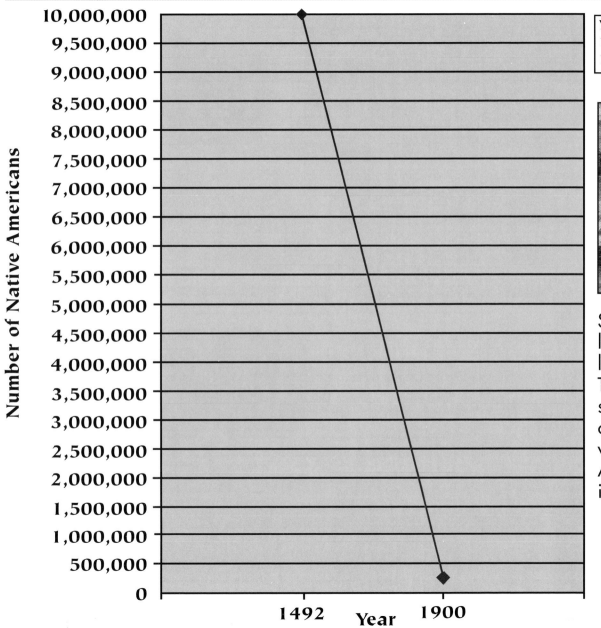

Year	NA Population
1492	10,000,000
1900	250,000

Number of Native Americans

10,000,000
9,500,000
9,000,000
8,500,000
8,000,000
7,500,000
7,000,000
6,500,000
6,000,000
5,500,000
5,000,000
4,500,000
4,000,000
3,500,000
3,000,000
2,500,000
2,000,000
1,500,000
1,000,000
500,000
0

1492   **Year**   1900

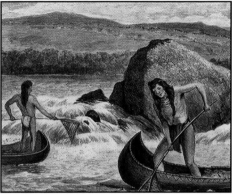

Some Native Americans who lived near waters sailed in long boats like this canoe. They used spears, or long sticks with metal ends, to catch fish. This hand-colored woodcut shows Native Americans fishing for salmon in the Columbia River.

NA Population

7

Concept Web:
Reasons for European Exploration

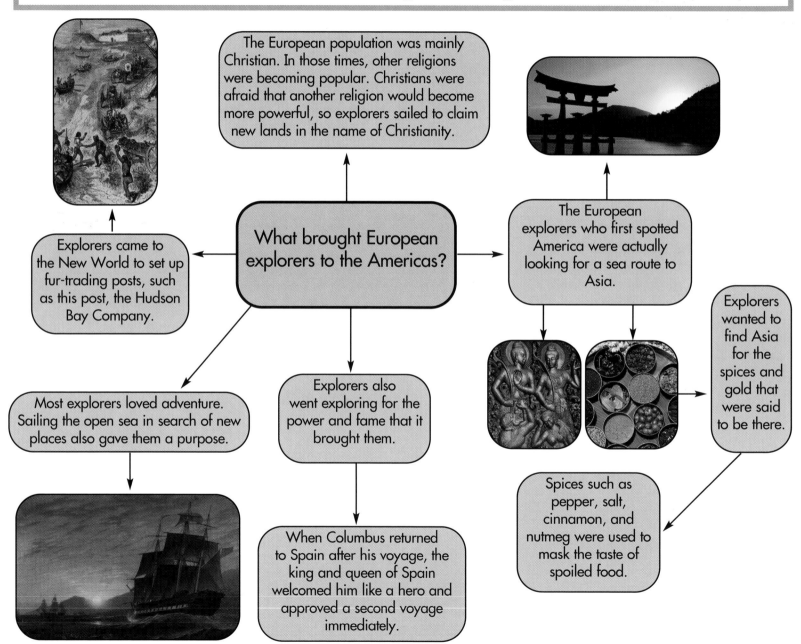

The European population was mainly Christian. In those times, other religions were becoming popular. Christians were afraid that another religion would become more powerful, so explorers sailed to claim new lands in the name of Christianity.

Explorers came to the New World to set up fur-trading posts, such as this post, the Hudson Bay Company.

What brought European explorers to the Americas?

The European explorers who first spotted America were actually looking for a sea route to Asia.

Explorers wanted to find Asia for the spices and gold that were said to be there.

Most explorers loved adventure. Sailing the open sea in search of new places also gave them a purpose.

Explorers also went exploring for the power and fame that it brought them.

Spices such as pepper, salt, cinnamon, and nutmeg were used to mask the taste of spoiled food.

When Columbus returned to Spain after his voyage, the king and queen of Spain welcomed him like a hero and approved a second voyage immediately.

Columbus's Voyage and Spanish Exploration

In 1492, Christopher Columbus sailed from Spain in search of a sea route to China. He hoped to find spices and gold. On October 12, Columbus landed on an island in the Bahamas, in North America. Thinking that he had reached the Indies, a group of islands near China, he called the people living on the island "Indians." The Europeans turned many of the native peoples they met into slaves. Many natives died from European **diseases**. In 1513, Ponce de León sailed to America's east coast searching for a magical spring of youth, but he discovered Florida instead. In 1519, Ferdinand Magellan's **voyage** around the world showed that Earth was round. These early voyages opened the door to European exploration and change in the Americas. Explorers returned home with wonderful stories of the New World, and their countries' governments planned for colonization.

A concept web arranges different ideas in a way that shows how they are connected to one main idea. The main idea is in the center of the web. This concept web shows the different reasons European explorers came to the Americas.

Early English, French, and Dutch Exploration

Like Spain, England, France, and Holland wanted to find a sea route to Asia. In 1497, England sent John Cabot sailing for Asia. He, too, ended up exploring North America. Because of this voyage, England later claimed all of North America's east coast. In 1524, France sent Giovanni da Verrazano to find Asia. As did others before him, he failed. Instead he found the harbor of present-day New York. While sailing for the Dutch in 1609, Henry Hudson uncovered the body of water now called the Hudson River. As did the Spanish government, the English, French, and Dutch governments began sending settlers to colonize the New World. Each country hoped that these colonies would bring it wealth and power. The French settled much of Canada. The English and the Dutch settled mostly on America's east coast.

Maps show you where certain places are located. This map uses different colored lines and shading to show the European exploration and settlement of the Americas. The key on the bottom of the page shows which colors stand for which countries. Notice that all of the lines have names and dates that tell you which explorer made this voyage, and in what year the voyage was made.

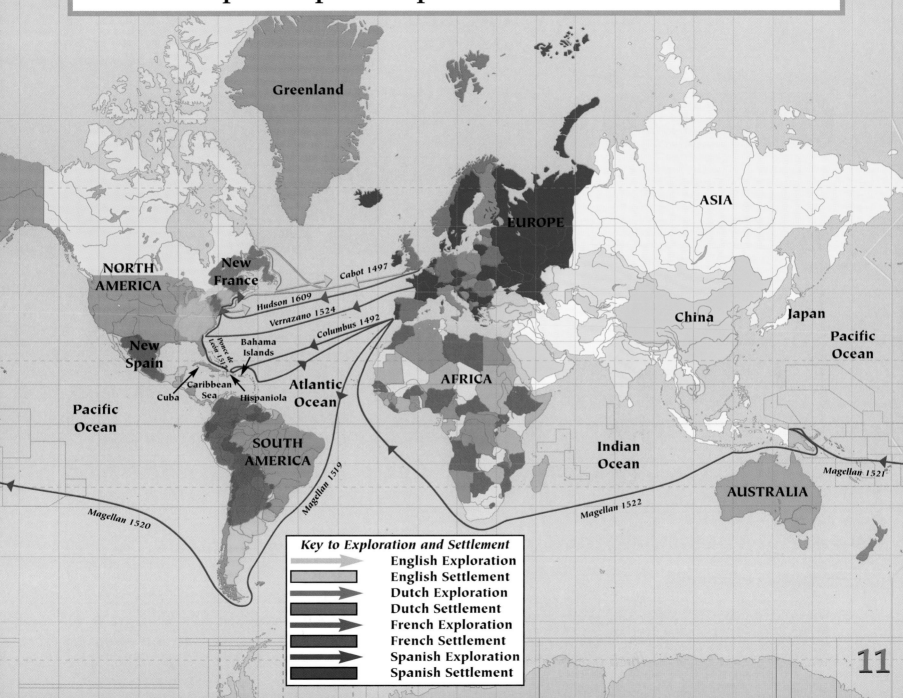

Map: European Exploration and Settlement

Greenland

NORTH AMERICA

New France

ASIA

EUROPE

Cabot 1497

Hudson 1609

Verrazano 1524

Columbus 1492

China

Japan

Pacific Ocean

New Spain

Ponce de Leon 1513

Bahama Islands

Cuba

Caribbean Sea

Hispaniola

Atlantic Ocean

AFRICA

Pacific Ocean

SOUTH AMERICA

Magellan 1519

Indian Ocean

AUSTRALIA

Magellan 1521

Magellan 1520

Magellan 1522

Key to Exploration and Settlement

English Exploration

English Settlement

Dutch Exploration

Dutch Settlement

French Exploration

French Settlement

Spanish Exploration

Spanish Settlement

11

Classifying Web:
Settlers Who Came to America

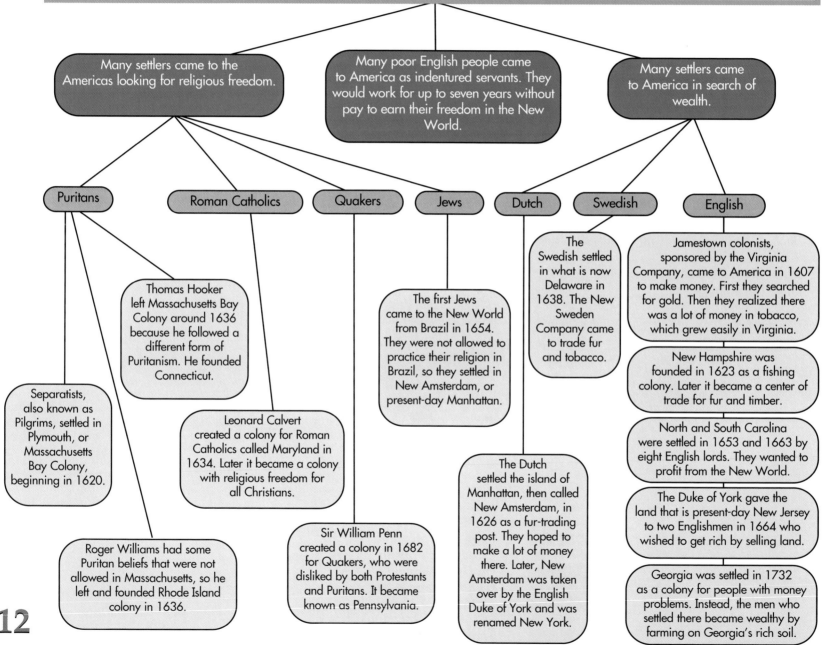

Many settlers came to the Americas looking for religious freedom.

Many poor English people came to America as indentured servants. They would work for up to seven years without pay to earn their freedom in the New World.

Many settlers came to America in search of wealth.

Puritans

Roman Catholics

Quakers

Jews

Dutch

Swedish

English

Thomas Hooker left Massachusetts Bay Colony around 1636 because he followed a different form of Puritanism. He founded Connecticut.

The first Jews came to the New World from Brazil in 1654. They were not allowed to practice their religion in Brazil, so they settled in New Amsterdam, or present-day Manhattan.

The Swedish settled in what is now Delaware in 1638. The New Sweden Company came to trade fur and tobacco.

Jamestown colonists, sponsored by the Virginia Company, came to America in 1607 to make money. First they searched for gold. Then they realized there was a lot of money in tobacco, which grew easily in Virginia.

Separatists, also known as Pilgrims, settled in Plymouth, or Massachusetts Bay Colony, beginning in 1620.

Leonard Calvert created a colony for Roman Catholics called Maryland in 1634. Later it became a colony with religious freedom for all Christians.

New Hampshire was founded in 1623 as a fishing colony. Later it became a center of trade for fur and timber.

North and South Carolina were settled in 1653 and 1663 by eight English lords. They wanted to profit from the New World.

The Dutch settled the island of Manhattan, then called New Amsterdam, in 1626 as a fur-trading post. They hoped to make a lot of money there. Later, New Amsterdam was taken over by the English Duke of York and was renamed New York.

The Duke of York gave the land that is present-day New Jersey to two Englishmen in 1664 who wished to get rich by selling land.

Roger Williams had some Puritan beliefs that were not allowed in Massachusetts, so he left and founded Rhode Island colony in 1636.

Sir William Penn created a colony in 1682 for Quakers, who were disliked by both Protestants and Puritans. It became known as Pennsylvania.

Georgia was settled in 1732 as a colony for people with money problems. Instead, the men who settled there became wealthy by farming on Georgia's rich soil.

12

The Early English Colonies

Many English colonists settled in the Americas. They all came for different reasons. Some settlers came for **religious** freedom. Some settlers came as **indentured servants** to escape poor living conditions. The first settlement, called Roanoke, was founded in 1585. It did not last. The first **surviving** colony, Jamestown, was settled in Virginia in 1607. The settlers learned how to hunt, farm, and fish from the local Native Americans. Without their help, the settlers would have died. As the colony grew, colonists took over Native American lands and hunting grounds for their tobacco farms. Slaves were brought to Virginia to work the tobacco fields. Jamestown's success made the birth of the United States possible. However, the way that the Europeans treated the native peoples and the Africans was **unjust**. The European way of life cost the Native Americans their homeland and the Africans their freedom.

Classifying webs show how different ideas or topics are connected to one another. This web shows the reasons different groups of people chose to settle in America. It tells you who came for religious reasons and who came for wealth, and where each group chose to settle.

The Slave Trade

Nearly 50 years before Columbus's voyage, Portugal explored the west coast of Africa. Portugal needed workers, so Portuguese explorers began **importing** Africans as slaves. By the mid-1500s, many European countries were **involved** in the slave trade. African slaves were first brought to America in 1619 by English colonists. The slave journey from Africa to the New World was called the Middle Passage. Ships sailed from Europe to Africa carrying goods such as guns, gunpowder, iron, and cloth. There the **cargo** was traded for Africans. The ships then sailed to America with human cargo. Hundreds of slaves were chained together and packed into tiny spaces on small ships. The dirty living conditions aboard the ships caused illness and death. The slaves who did survive this trip had a hard life ahead of them. Many slaves had lives filled with suffering and pain.

The graphic organizer to the right is a sequence chart. It shows a group of events, which occur in order, and have both a beginning and an end. This sequence chart shows the events that led to the rise of African slavery in the Americas and the transatlantic slave trade.

Sequence Chart:
The Rise of African Slavery

Portuguese explorers go to Africa in search of gold. They do not find gold. They return instead, with Africans. In Europe, the Africans are forced into slavery. They are traded for goods such as guns, cloth, and beads.

About 50 years later, Columbus, by chance, explores the Bahamas. This opens the door to European exploration of the Americas.

The Spanish colonize much of Central America and South America. They bring African slaves there to work on cotton and sugar plantations, or farms.

The English colonize much of what today is the United States. Many poor English folk come over as indentured servants. Africans are first brought to America as indentured servants by the English colonists of Virginia.

England's economy improves. White English people stop coming to work in America as indentured servants. The English colonists need workers for their farms, so they begin importing more slaves.

The English colonies grow. Southern cotton, rice, and tobacco plantations require many workers. Americans bring more Africans over as slaves on what is called the Middle Passage. The transatlantic slave trade begins.

Above: This map, created in 1743, shows the west coast of Africa. The picture in the corner shows native Africans working in their village. *Below:* This picture shows Europeans forcing Africans into slavery.

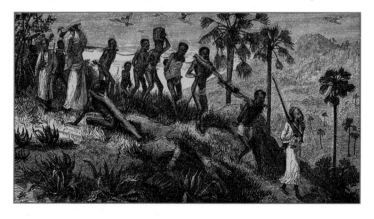

15

Chart: Four Major Explorers of New York State

Explorer	Country	Date and Voyage Goal	Part of NYS Discovered
Giovanni da Verrazano	France	In 1524, Verrazano sailed in search of a water passage, called the Northwest Passage, thought to go through North America to Asia.	Verrazano discovered the mouth of the New York Bay, or present-day Hudson River.
Jacques Cartier	France	In 1534, Cartier sailed in search of the Northwest Passage to Asia.	Cartier discovered the river that is called the St. Lawrence River.
Samuel de Champlain	France	In 1608, Champlain sailed to North America on a fur-trading trip.	Champlain explored the Atlantic coast and established the Canadian city of Quebec. Champlain explored the northern part of New York State.
Henry Hudson	Holland	In 1609, Hudson sailed in search of the Northwest Passage to Asia.	Hudson explored the Hudson River and the Hudson River valley, near Albany, NY.

This photograph of the Hudson River was taken in 1995. The river was named for Henry Hudson. The river was called Muhheakunnuk, or "great waters constantly in motion," by the Native Americans who had lived on its banks for years.

Three Worlds Meet in New York

In 1626, a Dutch settlement called New Amsterdam was established on the island known today as Manhattan. It is said that Peter Minuit, the governor of the colony, bought the island from the local Algonquin Indians for what amounts to $24 today. Native Americans did not believe that land could be owned by people. The Algonquins probably did not understand what they were agreeing to when they made the deal. Perhaps they thought that the settlers just wanted to borrow the land. New York's large harbor made trading a successful business. The Dutch set up a fur-trading post and immediately brought slaves to New Amsterdam to help with the work. Later, in 1664, the colony was taken over by the English and was renamed New York in honor of the Duke of York. New York grew to be one of the most successful and important colonies in the new American nation.

A chart is used to organize facts about several connected topics or ideas. This chart lists the four major explorers of New York State. It shows what countries they were from, when they sailed, what they were looking for, and what part of New York they explored.

Europeans and Native Americans

The colonists continued to establish new colonies in America. However, these lands were already **inhabited** by many Native Americans. In the beginning, the Native Americans were welcoming, and **introduced** the colonists to corn, potatoes, and tobacco. The colonists introduced the Native Americans to horses and guns for hunting. Colonists traded metal pots, knives, tools, and glass beads with the Native Americans for fur. The colonial population grew, and the Native Americans were forced to move farther west. Some groups, such as the Iroquois, refused to leave their land in New York, but in the end were forced out. Contact with the Europeans **exposed** Native Americans to diseases such as **smallpox**. Their bodies could not fight these diseases. Even the common cold and the flu were often deadly to them. Thousands of Native Americans died during these early years of settlement.

This is a cause-and-effect chart. The boxes on the left show different causes, usually events or occurrences. In the right-hand boxes are the effects, or things that happened as a result of the causes. This chart shows the effects of European exploration on the Native Americans.

Cause-and-Effect Chart:
What Happened to the Native Americans?

Cause

Effect

Cause	Effect
As English colonies grew, the colonists took over Native American lands for their own plantations.	Native Americans had to move farther west and north to lands without enough food, water, or shelter. Native Americans died on the long journeys to new lands
Native Americans had lived for thousands of years without contact with other people. Europeans brought diseases with them from other countries.	Native Americans were not able to fight off these diseases, and thousands of Native Americans died from them.
Many Native Americans died in battles with the colonists. Native Americans tried to fight for their land and their homes when the colonists took over. However, they often lost because the colonists had guns.	The Native American population declined, or went down, greatly in the years following the English colonization of America. It fell from a population in the 10 millions to one of a few hundred thousand.

Despite the many problems between the Native Americans and the Europeans, some members of these two cultures became friends. Many groups of Native Americans lived peacefully with the European settlers. Europeans traded metal, guns, and other items from Europe for fur. Native Americans taught the Europeans how to farm and fish.

19

Pie Chart: African Slave Populations in the Colonies in 1790

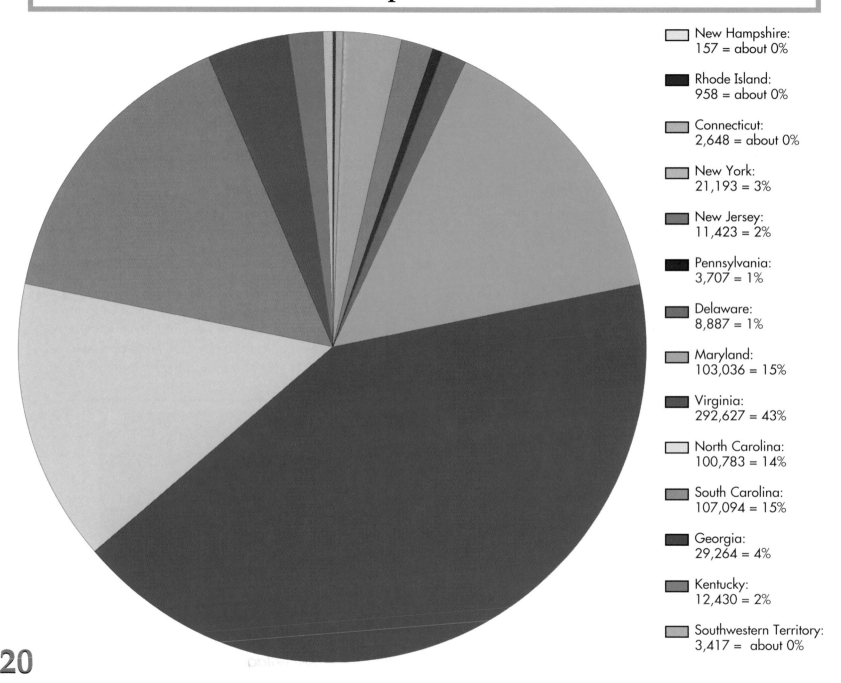

New Hampshire:
157 = about 0%

Rhode Island:
958 = about 0%

Connecticut:
2,648 = about 0%

New York:
21,193 = 3%

New Jersey:
11,423 = 2%

Pennsylvania:
3,707 = 1%

Delaware:
8,887 = 1%

Maryland:
103,036 = 15%

Virginia:
292,627 = 43%

North Carolina:
100,783 = 14%

South Carolina:
107,094 = 15%

Georgia:
29,264 = 4%

Kentucky:
12,430 = 2%

Southwestern Territory:
3,417 = about 0%

Slavery in the Colonies

The colonies grew in population and in area. By the 1660s, England's living conditions had improved, and fewer indentured servants came to the colonies. This new lack of labor caused the colonists to use more slaves than they had before. In the northern colonies, Africans were used as house servants or in trade work. The southern colonies had the largest slave population. The crops grown in the south, such as tobacco, rice, and cotton, required many workers. As the farms grew, the need for labor increased.

Southern slaves were treated poorly and often beaten. Family members were separated and sold to different owners. Africans were not allowed education or the right to practice their African beliefs. By 1709, Virginia, Maryland, and South Carolina each had more than 10,000 slaves. The number of Africans forced into slavery in the colonies continued to grow during the 1800s.

Pie charts show percentages. Each slice of the pie stands for a part, or fraction, of 100. This pie chart shows the percentages of slaves in the 13 colonies and the Southwestern Territory. Some colonies had so few slaves, compared to other colonies, that their percentage appears to be zero.

The New Americas

In 1492, Columbus's men yelled "tierra," or "land," from their ship on the Atlantic when they spotted the Americas. Since then, the Americas have grown and changed in many different ways. Many different cultures made this change possible. Today cities and lakes are named for Native American tribes to remind Americans of their country's history. Native American jewelry, music, and sports have become a part of today's American culture. Lacrosse, a popular school sport in the United States, was first played by the Native Americans. The Europeans brought wealth, promise, and growth to America. They **influenced** American government, language, **customs**, food, and building styles. African influences can be seen in music, such as jazz and blues, in language in the South, and in food in both the southern United States and the Caribbean. The United States would not exist today without the hard work and bravery of all three of the worlds that came together there hundreds of years ago.

Glossary

cargo (KAR-goh) The load of goods carried by an airplane, a ship, or an automobile.

clashed (KLASHD) Had strong disagreements, did not get along.

colonization (kah-lih-nih-ZAY-shun) The settling of a new land and the claiming of it for the government of another country.

contact (KON-takt) The touching or meeting of people or things.

continent (KON-tin-ent) One of Earth's seven large land masses.

cultures (KUL-churz) Beliefs, practices, and arts of groups of people.

customs (KUS-tumz) Practices common to many people in an area or a social class.

diseases (duh-ZEEZ-ez) Illnesses or sicknesses.

explorers (ek-SPLOR-urz) People who travel and look for new land.

exposed (ek-SPOHZD) Put in the way of something harmful.

graphic organizers (GRA-fik OR-guh-ny-zerz) Charts, graphs, and pictures that sort facts and ideas and make them clear.

importing (IM-port-ing) Bringing in from another country.

indentured servants (in-DEN-churd SER-vints) People who have worked for another person for a fixed amount of time for payment of travel or living costs.

influenced (IN-floo-ensd) To have swayed others without using force.

inhabited (in-HA-bit-ed) To have lived in a certain place.

introduced (in-truh-DOOSD) To have brought into use, knowledge, or notice.

involved (in-VOLVD) To be kept busy by something.

New World (NOO WURLD) North America and South America.

religious (ree-LIH-jus) Having to do with a faith, a system of beliefs.

smallpox (SMOL-poks) A sickness that leaves marks on the skin and often causes death.

surviving (sur-VYV-ing) Continuing to exist.

unjust (un-JUST) Not fair.

voyage (VOY-ij) A journey by water.

Index

A
Africans, 13–14, 21
Algonquin Indians, 17
Aztecs, 6

B
Bering Land Bridge, 5

C
Cabot, John, 10
colony(ies), 10, 13, 17–18,
    21
Columbus, Christopher, 9, 14,
    22

E
Europeans, 5–6, 9, 13, 18,
    22
explorers, 5, 9–10, 14

H
Hudson, Henry, 10

I
Incas, 6
indentured servants, 13, 21
Iroquois, 18

J
Jamestown, 13

M
Magellan, Ferdinand, 9
Maya, 6
Middle Passage, 14
Minuit, Peter, 17

N
Native Americans, 6, 13,
    17–18, 22

New World, 5, 9–10,
    13–14
New York, 10, 17–18

P
Ponce de León, 9

R
Roanoke, 13

S
settlers, 10, 13, 17
slaves, 5, 9, 13–14, 21

V
Verrazano, Giovanni da, 10

Web Sites

Due to the changing nature of Internet links, PowerKids Press has developed an online list of Web sites related to the subject of this book. This site is updated regularly. Please use this link to access the list: www.powerkidslinks.com/goss/threewor/